FRUITVILLE PUBLIC LIBRARY

100 COBURN ROAD
SARASOTA, FL 34240

A BEACON ✶ BIOGRAPHY

Michelle Obama

Tamra B. Orr

PURPLE TOAD

Printing   1   2   3   4   5   6   7   8   9

A Beacon Biography

Angelina Jolie	Kevin Durant
Anthony Davis	Lorde
Ben Simmons	Malala
Big Time Rush	Maria von Trapp
Bill Nye	Markus "Notch" Persson, Creator of Minecraft
Cam Newton	Meghan Markle
Carly Rae Jepsen	Michelle Obama
Carson Wentz	Millie Bobby Brown
Chadwick Boseman	Misty Copeland
Daisy Ridley	Mo'ne Davis
Drake	Muhammad Ali
Ed Sheeran	Neil deGrasse Tyson
Ellen DeGeneres	Oprah Winfrey
Elon Musk	Peyton Manning
Ezekiel Elliott	Robert Griffin III (RG3)
Gal Gadot	Stephen Colbert
Harry Styles of One Direction	Stephen Curry
Jennifer Lawrence	Tom Holland
Joel Embiid	Zendaya
John Boyega	

Library of Congress Cataloging-in-Publication Data
Orr, Tamra B.
   Michelle Obama / Written by Tamra B. Orr.
      p. cm.
Includes bibliographic, references, glossary, and index.
ISBN 9781624694264
1. Obama, Michelle. 1964- — Juvenile literature. 2. United States First Lady — Biography — Juvenile literature. 3. African American Female Lawyers — Juvenile literature. I. Series: A Beacon Biography

E909.O24 B66 A45 2019
973.932092
[B]

Library of Congress Control Number: 2018943800

eBook ISBN: 9781624694257

ABOUT THE AUTHOR: Tamra B. Orr is a full-time author who lives in the Pacific Northwest with her family. She graduated from Ball State University in Muncie, Indiana. She has written more than 500 books about everything from historical events and career choices to controversial issues and celebrity biographies. On those rare occasions that she is not writing a book, she is reading one. She is a big fan of the Obamas and loved the chance to learn more about Michelle.

PUBLISHER'S NOTE: This story has not been authorized or endorsed by Michelle Obama.

CONTENTS

The 2008 Democratic National Convention gave Michelle Obama the chance to show Americans just what kind of First Lady she could be.

Turning It Around

The pressure was intense.

The Pepsi Center in Denver, Colorado, was full, with thousands of people in the audience. They had come to the Democratic National Convention to cheer on their nominee, Barack Obama, for president of the United States. It was opening night of the four-day event. The headline speaker was Michelle Obama, the country's future first lady.

It was a tough moment for Michelle. In recent weeks, she had been criticized by the Republicans and the press. In a speech from earlier in the year, she had said that she was quite proud of her country—for the first time in her adult life. It was not long before she was labeled unpatriotic. Her approval rating, a number that reflects how many Americans like or approve of what a politician is doing, had dropped to

Michelle Obama's speech focused on values, hard work, and hope.

a disappointing 35 percent. Now she was about to face a huge crowd. She wanted to turn things around. She wanted her audience to support Barack. She also wanted them to see her as a great potential first lady.

The first thing she did was connect to the audience. "I come here as a wife who loves my husband and believes he will be an extraordinary president," she stated. "I come here as a mom whose girls are the heart of my heart and the center of my world—they're the first thing I think about when I wake up in the morning, and the last thing I think about when I go to bed at night. . . . Their future—and all our children's future—is my stake in this election." She emphasized how she and Barack had overcome the odds to reach the White House by listening to their hopes instead of their fears. She then added, ". . . we decided to stop doubting and to start dreaming . . . in this great country—where a girl from the South Side of Chicago can go to college and law school, and the son of a single mother from Hawaii can go all the way to the White House—we committed ourselves to building the world as it should be."

When her speech ended, everyone rose to their feet, applauding. Michelle had done it. Soon after her speech, her approval rating shot up to 65 percent. It stayed there for the next eight years.

Michelle Obama served as the nation's first lady for two terms. During those years, she worked to prove she was patriotic. Many historians predict she will be considered one of the most beloved, respected, and effective first ladies in history.

Despite their busy schedules, President Barack Obama and First Lady Michelle Obama always made time for their daughters Sasha (left) and Malia.

The Obamas reflect on their lives in and out of Chicago, remembering how hard they worked to reach the White House.

Chapter 2

Simple Beginnings

Michelle LaVaughn Robinson's childhood was a simple one—but a loving one. When she joined the family on January 17, 1964, she had an older brother waiting for her. Craig was 21 months old when she born. As she grew, many people thought the two were twins. "I was just a typical South Side little black girl," says Michelle. "Not a whole lot of money. Going to a circus once a year was a big deal. Getting pizza on Friday was a treat. Summers were long and fun."

Michelle and Craig had daily chores. They cleaned the bathroom, scrubbed the sinks, and mopped the floors. They were allowed to watch one hour of television a day. As often as possible, Michelle watched the show *The Brady Bunch*. It was her favorite program, and she memorized most of the episodes.

Many evenings at the Robinson house were spent playing favorite games like Chinese checkers, Monopoly, and Scrabble. Both Craig and Michelle were reading by the age of four. Both skipped second grade. During her 2008 convention speech, Michelle said, "At 6-foot-6, I've often felt like Craig was looking down on me . . . literally. But the truth is, both when we were kids and today, he wasn't looking down on me. He was watching over me."

Michelle's father, Fraser Robinson, worked for the Chicago Water Department. He was a city pump operator. He was diagnosed with multiple sclerosis when he was in his 30s. In 2008's convention speech, Michelle spoke about her father with great love. "My dad was our rock . . . our provider, our champion, our hero," she stated. "As he got sicker, it got harder for him to walk, it took him longer to get dressed in the morning. But if he was in pain, he never let on. He never stopped smiling and laughing—even while struggling to button his shirt, even while using two canes to get himself across the room to give my mom a kiss. He just woke up a little earlier and worked a little harder."

Marian Robinson, Michelle's mother, was an at-home mom. In 2009, Michelle described how her mother inspired her. "My mother's love has always been a sustaining force for our family, and one of my greatest joys is seeing her integrity, her compassion, and her intelligence reflected in my own daughters." When Michelle and her family moved into the White House, her mother joined them.

In 2009, Marian Robinson joined her daughter Michelle in handing out treats for Halloween.

From 1970 to 1977, Michelle went to Bryn Mawr Elementary School. Thanks to her high grades, by sixth grade she was invited to attend Whitney M. Young Magnet School. It was the area's first school for gifted students. Michelle rode the bus or train for two hours to get to school

Princeton grad

every morning. It took another two hours to ride back home. Michelle learned French at Young. She also took several high-level science courses. In 1981, she graduated as the school's salutatorian.

When Michelle looks back on being a student, she admits she wishes she could have done a few things differently. She told *People*, "I was afraid of not knowing the answer in class and looking stupid, or worried about what some boy thought of me, or wondering whether the other girls liked my clothes or my hair. . . . I would love to go back in time and tell my younger self, 'Michelle, these middle and high school years are just a tiny blip in your life, and all the slights and embarrassments and heartaches, all those times you got that one question wrong on that test—none of that is important in the scheme of things.' "

After high school, Michelle enrolled at Princeton University. She attended from 1981 to 1985, earning a degree in Sociology and a minor in African American Studies. While there, she started an after-school reading program for children of university workers. Next, she went to Harvard Law School, where she spent many hours working with a public service law bureau. She helped people who needed a lawyer but could not afford one.

Michelle graduated in 1988. She took a job as an associate attorney at the Chicago law firm Sidley Austin. Little did she know that soon someone who was going to change the course of her life was about to walk through the door.

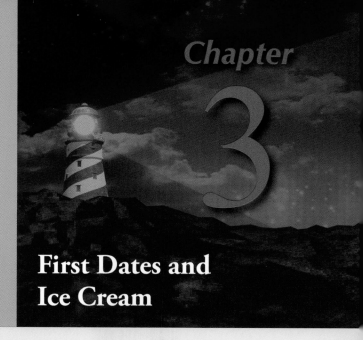

From the first date, Michelle and Barack knew they had met their match—in every way.

First Dates and Ice Cream

One day in June 1989, while Michelle was working at Sidley Austin, a young law student named Barack Obama walked into the law office. He was there to work as a summer intern, directly with Michelle Robinson. Years later, in an interview with Oprah Winfrey, Barack recalled what happened next: "I remember being struck by how tall and beautiful she was. She, I have since learned, was pleasantly surprised to see that my nose and ears weren't quite as enormous as they looked in the photo I'd submitted for the firm directory." He admitted he asked her out again and again. She kept saying no. " 'I'm your adviser,' she said. 'It's not appropriate.' Finally, I offered to quit my job, and at last she relented," he stated. "On our first date, I treated her to the finest ice cream Baskin-Robbins had to offer, our dinner table doubling as the curb. I kissed her, and it tasted like chocolate."

In August 2012, a plaque was put up in front of the ice cream shop to honor that first kiss. In 2016, a movie called *Southside with You* was made about that famous first date. Starring Parker Sawyers as Barack and Tika Sumpter as Michelle, the movie was filmed in many parts of Chicago. *Southside with You* was a hit, and hailed by many as "gorgeously romantic."

Michelle and Barack were engaged in 1991. Michelle tells the story: "We were at a restaurant having dinner to celebrate the fact that he [Barack] had finished the bar. Then the waiter came over with the dessert and a tray. And there was the ring. And I was completely shocked." The two were married on October 3, 1992, at the Trinity United Church of Christ in Chicago.

In 2009, when explaining what had drawn her to Barack, Michelle said, "[What] struck me when I first met Barack was that even though he had this funny name, even though he'd grown up all the way across the continent in Hawaii, his family was so much like mine. He was raised by grandparents who were working-class folks just like my parents, and by a single mother who struggled to pay the bills just like

President Barack Obama, First Lady Michelle Obama, and daughters Sasha and Malia, center, with their extended family , January 20, 2013. The First Family poses with (from left): Craig Robinson, Leslie Robinson, Avery Robinson, Marian Robinson, Akinyi Manners, Auma Obama, Maya Soetoro-Ng, Konrad Ng, and in front, Savita Ng and Suhaila Ng.

The President and First Lady—both wearing smiles—dance at the 2009 inaugural ball.

we did. Like my family," she continued, "they scrimped and saved so that he could have opportunities they never had themselves. And Barack and I were raised with so many of the same values: that you work hard for what you want in life; that your word is your bond and you do what you say you're going to do; that you treat people with dignity and respect, even if you don't know them, and even if you don't agree with them."

When Barack and Michelle began dating, she was a little worried. He was poor, drove an old car, and wore rather shabby clothes. As Michelle told the *Hyde Park Herald*, "[H]e had no money; he was really broke. He wasn't ever going to try to impress me with things. His wardrobe was kind of

Barack and Michelle share a laugh during the inaugural parade in an official car for the president.

cruddy. . . . His first car had so much rust that there was a rusted hole in the passenger door. You could see the ground when you were driving. He loved that car. It would shake ferociously when it would start up. I thought, 'This brother is not interested in ever making a dime.' " It never entered her mind that her future husband had any interest in a political career.

Michelle Obama plants an organic garden on the White House lawn with a group of fifth-graders. The White House kitchen would use the produce in state dinners. The garden was part of Michelle's Let's Move Campaign.

Michelle was extremely ambitious both before and after she married Barack. In 1991, she worked as an assistant to Chicago Mayor Richard M. Daley. After that, she worked for the Chicago Office of Public Allies. There she started a leadership training program to help young people develop skills for getting jobs within the community. In 1996, she joined the University of Chicago as Associate Dean of Student Services. By 2002, she was Executive Director of Community Relations for the University of Chicago Hospitals; and three years later, she was Vice President for Community and External Affairs at the University of Chicago Medical Center.

In 2006, Michelle was listed as one of the 25 most inspiring women in the world by *Essence* magazine. The following year, Harvard included her in its 100 Most Influential Alumni list. She was featured on the cover of several fashion magazines as being one of the best-dressed women in the country. As busy as she was, Michelle had time to do two additional things: She became a mother, and she realized that her husband's dreams were headed in a political direction.

In 1996, Barack Obama became the Democratic Senator for Illinois. He was reelected twice. In 2004, he was elected to the United States

Congress. Three years later, he announced he would run for U.S. president. During those years, he had also become a father. Daughter Malia was born in July 1998 and daughter Natasha (Sasha) was born in June 2001.

Immediately, Michelle's top priority became her children. Becoming the country's First Family was frightening for her. How would it affect her daughters? What would it be like to grow up in the national spotlight?

Despite her misgivings, Michelle went on the campaign trail with Barack in 2007. "My first priority will always be to make sure that our girls are healthy and grounded," she stated on her Our White House page. "Then I want to help other families get the support they need, not just to survive, but to thrive." In her Colorado speech, she made it clear that she was 100 percent behind her husband. When he won the presidential election in 2008, Michelle became the First Lady of the United States, or FLOTUS. Barack was reelected in 2012, so she remained FLOTUS for four more years.

During her time in the White House, Michelle worked very hard to support and improve the lives of all Americans. She volunteered at homeless shelters and in soup kitchens. She spoke in countless public schools. Concerned about the problem of childhood obesity, Michelle started the Let's Move fitness program. It encouraged young people to try new sports and stay active. The First Lady, along with a classroom of local fifth graders, planted a 1,100-square-foot garden of fresh herbs and vegetables behind the White House. She also had beehives installed on the South Lawn. In 2012, she published a book about it titled *American Grown: The Story of the White House Kitchen Garden and Gardens Across America.*

As Lauren Wright, political scientist and author, told *NBC News*, "Michelle Obama always approached the topic of health care from the perspective of a mom, of a family, of someone who cares about the generation of kids that are going to come after the Obama administration." In 2014, Michelle founded the Reach Higher organization to encourage students around the world to continue their education past high school.

In addition to all of her projects, Michelle also became one of the first first ladies to use social media to connect with Americans. She posted online, participated in a number of television sketches, danced on *Ellen* to promote exercise, and even handed out the Oscar for Best

Michelle was one of the first first ladies to become a familiar face outside of the White House. Her sense of humor shone through in her appearances, such as when she joined Ellen DeGeneres on her talk show.

*Michelle stunned the audience when she showed up, via video screen, to present the Oscar for Best Picture to the producers of **Argo**. She honored movies that "lift spirits, broaden our minds, and transport us to places we never imagined."*

Picture at the 2013 Academy Awards. In a 2012 speech at the Democratic National Convention, Michelle stated, "Every day, the people I meet inspire me, every day they make me proud, every day they remind me how blessed we are to live in the greatest nation on earth. Serving as your first lady is an honor and a privilege."

There is little doubt that Barack believes Michelle was one of the most important keys to his successful presidency. In his State of the Union Address in 2010, he said, "If you were going to list the 100 most popular things that I have done as president, being married to Michelle

Obama is number one." A year later, he told Oprah Winfrey in an interview, "Obviously I couldn't have done anything that I've done without Michelle. You were asking earlier what keeps me sane, what keeps me balanced, what allows me to deal with the pressure. It is this young lady right here. . . . Not only has she been a great first lady, she is just my rock. I count on her in so many ways every single day."

As part of her Make a Difference program, Michelle goes barefoot and plays vocabulary-building hopscotch with orphans in India.

Both Barack and Michelle have been very active in civil rights issues. Here they celebrate the 50th anniversary of the famous civil rights march from Selma to Mongomery, Alabama.

Beyond the White House

In late 2016, the Obamas' time in the White House came to an end. A number of Americans hoped to see Michelle move from First Lady to Madam President. Michelle quickly put that rumor to rest. She told Oprah Winfrey, "Running for president? No. If I were interested in it, I'd say it. I don't believe in playing games. It's not something I would do, but it also speaks to the fact that people don't really understand how [being in the White House] is. I mean, the next family that comes in here, every person in that family, every child, every grandchild, their lives will be turned upside down in a way that no American really understands. . . . It is a truth, an actuality, that there is a weight to it."

No longer being FLOTUS did not mean Michelle would not keep busy, however. "I will take the same approach leaving as I did coming in," she told *Vogue* magazine. "I won't know until I'm there. I've never been the former first lady of the United States of America before, but I will always be engaged in some way in public service and public life."

In 2016, both Barack and Michelle Obama returned to the campaign trail to support Hillary Clinton for U.S. president. In July, Michelle was once again the keynote speaker for the Democratic National Convention. She told the audience, "I wake up every morning in a house that was built by slaves, and I watch my daughters, two beautiful, intelligent, black young women, playing with their dogs on the White House lawn. And because of Hillary Clinton, my daughters, and all our sons and daughters, now take for granted that a woman can be president of the United States."

On January 2017, Michelle made her last official speech at the White House as the nation's first lady. She had an important message to share. "I want our young people to know that they matter, that they belong," she stated. "So don't be afraid. You hear me, young people? Don't be afraid. Be focused. Be determined. Be hopeful. Be

Clearly, there is no hurdle that Michelle cannot jump—even if it is just a rope during Nickelodeon's Worldwide Day of Play.

empowered. Empower yourself with a good education. Then get out there and use that education to build a country worthy of your boundless promise. Lead by example with hope; never fear."

Now that their White House days are behind them, the Obamas are spending their time traveling around the world, speaking to audiences at universities and organizations, and even writing their memoirs. Michelle has continued to attend events that encourage young people to further their education, as well as those that promote good health and nutrition. She and Barack plan to keep active because, as she stated in *Newsweek*, "We're not gone.

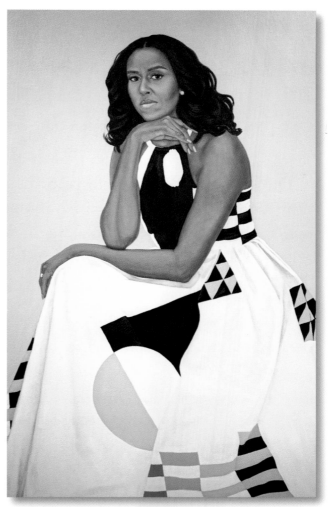

Michelle Obama's official portrait as First Lady was painted by Amy Sherald and it met with the couple's full approval. Barack thanked Sherald for "spectacularly capturing the grace and beauty and intelligence and charm . . . of the woman I love."

We're just breathing, y'all." Whatever direction she goes next, there is no doubt that Michelle will keep busy trying to make the world a better place—just as she always has.

1964	Michelle LaVaughn Robinson is born in Chicago, Illinois, on January 17.
1970–1977	She attends Bryn Mawr Elementary School.
1977–1981	She attends Whitney M. Young Magnet School.
1981–1985	She attends Princeton University, taking courses in sociology and African-American studies.
1985–1988	She attends Harvard Law School.
1988–1991	Michelle works at Sidley Austin law offices.
1989	She meets Barack Obama.
1991	She and Barack Obama are engaged; Michelle begins working for Chicago Mayor Richard M. Daley.
1992	Michelle and Barack Obama marry in October.
1993	Michelle works as Executive Director for the Chicago Office of Public Allies.
1996	She is named Associate Dean of Student Services at University of Chicago. Barack begins his political career as Democratic Senator for Illinois.
1998	Daughter Malia is born.
2001	Daughter Natasha (Sasha) is born.
2002	Michelle Obama works as Executive Director of Community Relations at University of Chicago Hospitals.
2005	She works as Vice President for Community and External Affairs at University of Chicago Medical Center.
2006	*Essence* magazine lists Michelle Obama as one of the world's 25 most inspiring women.
2007	She travels on the presidential campaign trail with Barack. She is named one of the Harvard 100.

2008–2016   As first lady, she establishes the Let's Move and Reach Higher campaigns. She promotes community gardening by reestablishing the White House gardens, growing produce for state dinners and other White House functions.

2012   A plaque of her first kiss with Barack Obama is displayed outside an ice cream store in Chicago. She publishes a book on gardening.

2016   The biographical film *Southside with You* is released.

2017   She continues to promote her causes of higher education, women's empowerment, and healthy choices around the country.

2018   DeKalb County, Georgia, renames a 3.8-mile trail after Michelle Obama in honor of her Let's Move campaign.

Books

Edwards, Roberta. *Michelle Obama: Mom in Chief/Primera dama y primera mama.* Madrid, Spain: Altea, 2010.

Stine, Megan. *Who Is Michelle Obama?* New York: Penguin Workshop, 2013.

Taylor-Butler, Christine. *Michelle Obama (A True Book).* New York: Children's Press, 2015.

Weatherford, Carole B. *Michelle Obama: First Mom.* New York: Two Lions, 2014.

Works Consulted

Bains, Pahull. "6 Things to Know About Barack and Michelle Obama's Official Portraits." Fashion, February 12, 2018. https://fashionmagazine.com/culture/barack-michelle-obamas-official-portraits/

Brinlee, Morgan. "11 Barack Obama Quotes about Michelle, Because We All Need Something to Believe In." *Bustle*, December 26, 2016. https://www.bustle.com/p/11-barack-obama-quotes-about-michelle-because-we-all-need-something-to-believe-in-26271

Drabold, Will. "Read Michelle Obama's Emotional Speech at the Democratic Convention." *Time*, July 26, 2016. http://time.com/4421538/democratic-convention-michelle-obama-transcript/

Evans, Kelley. "Passionate and Emotional: Michelle Obama's Final Speech as First Lady." *The Undefeated*, January 6, 2017. https://theundefeated.com/features/passionate-and-emotional-michelle-obamas-final-speech-as-first-lady/

"Job Well Done, First Lady! 16 Accomplishments of Michelle Obama." Black Doctor.org, n.d. https://blackdoctor.org/483712/job-well-done-first-lady-16-accomplishments-of-michelle-obama/

"Michelle Obama: Advice to My Younger Self." *People*, October 12, 2014. http://people.com/celebrity/michelle-obama-advice-to-my-younger-self/

Obama, Barack. "My First Date with Michelle." *Oprah*, n.d. http://www.oprah.com/world/barack-and-michelle-obamas-first-date-famous-firsts/all%20-%20ixzz552xJ00Yc

Obama, Barack. "State of the Union Speech." *Politico*, January 27, 2010. https://www.politico.com/story/2010/01/obamas-state-of-the-union-address-032111

Obama, Michelle. "Convention Speech." NPR: Oregon Public Broadcasting, August 25, 2008. https://www.npr.org/templates/story/story.php?storyId=93963863

Schwarz, Sam. "What Michelle Obama Has Been Up to Since Leaving the White House." *Newsweek*, December 29, 2017.

Silva, Daniella. "Michelle Obama: The Historic Legacy of the Nation's First Black First Lady." *NBC News*, January 6, 2017. https://www.nbcnews.com/storyline/president-obama-the-legacy/michelle-obama-historic-legacy-nation-s-first-black-first-lady-n703506

Swanson, Lorraine. " 'Southside with You' Chronicles Barack and Michelle Obama's Steamy First Date." *Chicago Patch*, August 23, 2016. https://patch.com/illinois/chicago/southside-you-chronicles-barack-michelle-obamas-steamy-first-date

Travers, Peter. " 'Southside with You' Review: Romantic Indie Recreates When Barack Met Michelle." *Rolling Stone*, August 24, 2017. https://www.rollingstone.com/movies/reviews/southside-with-you-movie-review-w435489

White House. "Our White House Looking In, Looking Out: Michelle Robinson Obama." White House.org, n.d. http://ourwhitehouse.org/michelle-robinson-obama/

Zakarin, Jordan. "Michelle Obama Makes Surprise Oscars Appearance, Reads Best Picture." The Hollywood Reporter, February 24, 2013.https://www.hollywoodreporter.com/news/michelle-obama-at-oscars-2013-424051

On the Internet

Kiddle: "Michelle Obama"
    https://kids.kiddle.co/Michelle_Obama

Michelle Obama's "Let's Move"
    https://letsmove.obamawhitehouse.archives.gov/

Mr. Nussbaum: "Michelle Obama"
    http://mrnussbaum.com/michelle-obama/

GLOSSARY

alumni (uh-LUM-neye)—Former students.

ambitious (am-BIH-shus)—Having many goals.

bar—The qualifying test to become a lawyer.

FLOTUS (FLOH-tus)—The shortened form of *First Lady of the United States.*

integrity (in-TEG-rih-tee)—Honesty or truthfulness; behaving according to one's beliefs.

memoirs (MEM-wahrs)—Written memories of one's life.

multiple sclerosis (MUL-tih-pul skler-OH-sis)—A disease of the nervous system.

nominee (nah-mih-NEE)—Someone who is officially proposed for a specific job or position.

obesity (oh-BEE-sih-tee)—The condition of being extremely fat or overweight.

salutatorian (sah-lyoo-tah-TOR-ee-un)—The second highest-scoring student in a graduating class.

unpatriotic (un-pay-tree-AH-tik)—Not proud of or loyal to one's country.